# THE USBORNE
# FIRST THOUSAND WORDS
## IN FRENCH
### With easy pronunciation guide

Heather Amery

Illustrated by Stephen Cartwright

Revised edition edited by Nicole Irving
and designed by Andy Griffin

French language consultant: Lorraine Sharp

Scholastic Inc.

New York    Toronto    London    Auckland    Sydney

On every big picture across two pages,
there is a little yellow duck to look for.
Can you find it?

# About this book

This book is for everyone who is starting to learn French. By looking at the small, labeled pictures, it will be easy to learn the words. You can also look at the large central picture and try to recall words for things. This helps to make the words stick in your mind, and it is also lots of fun. Seeing things in a scene will also help you to remember them.

### Masculine and feminine words

When you look at French words for things such as "table" or "man", you will see that they have **le**, **la** or **l'** in front of them. This is because all French words for things and people are either masculine or feminine. **Le** is the word for "the" in front of a masculine word, **la** is "the" in front of a feminine word, and you use **l'** in front of words that begin with "a", "e", "i", "o" or "u". In front of words that are plural (more than one, such as "tables" or "men"), the French word for "the" is **les**.

All the labels in this book show words for things with **le**, **la**, **l'** or **les**. Always learn them with this little word.

### Looking at French words

A few French words have accents. These are signs that are written over or under some letters. Usually they are over the letter "e", and they change the way you say the letter.

### Saying French words

The best way to learn how to say French words is to listen to a French speaker and repeat what you hear. To help you, though, in the word list at the back of the book, you will find an easy pronunciation guide for each French word.

## About this revised edition

This edition brings new life to an enormously popular book. The book has been redesigned to give even clearer pictures and labels, and there are many brand-new illustrations by Stephen Cartwright. The book has also been brought up to date, so that it now includes objects which have made their way into everyday life in recent years.

# La maison

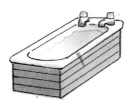

la baignoire

le savon

le robinet

le papier hygiénique

la brosse à dents

l'eau

les toilettes

l'éponge

le lavabo

la douche

la serviette

le lit

## La salle de bains

## Le salon

le dentifrice

la radio

le coussin

le CD

la moquette

le canapé

4

 chaise

 la couette

 le peigne

 le drap

 la descente de lit

 l'armoire

 l'oreiller

# la chambre

 la commode

 le miroir

 la brosse à cheveux

 la lampe

# l'entrée

 les posters

 le portemanteau

 le téléphone

 le radiateur

 la cassette vidéo

 le journal

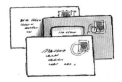 la table

 les lettres

l'escalier

5

# La cuisine

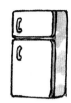

le réfrigérateur

les verres

la pendule

le tabouret

les petites cuillères

l'interrupteur

le paquet
de lessive

la clé

la porte

l'évier

l'aspirateur

les casseroles

les fourchettes

le tablier

la planche à
repasser

les ordures

la bouilloire

les couteaux

le balai à franges

le chiffon

les carreaux

le balai

le lave-linge

la pelle à ordures

le tiroir

les soucoupes

la poêle

la cuisinière

les cuillères en bois

les assiettes

le fer à repasser

le torchon

les tasses

les allumettes

la brosse

les bols

le placard

la brouette

la ruche

l'escargot

les briques

le pigeon

la bêche

la coccinelle

la poubelle

les graines

l'appentis

# Le jardin

l'arrosoir

le ver de terre

les fleurs

le tourniquet

la binette

la guêpe

l'abeille

le déplantoir

l'os

la haie

la fourche

la tondeuse

le chemin

les feuilles

l'arbre

la fumée

la chenille

le râteau

le nid

les bâtons

la serre

l'herbe

le landau

l'échelle

le feu

le tuyau d'arrosage

# L'atelier

l'étau

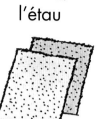
le papier de verre

la perceuse

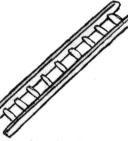
l'échelle

la scie

la sciure

le calendrier

la boîte à outils

les vis

le tournevis

la planche

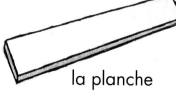
les copeaux

le canif

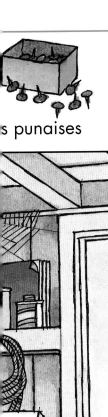
s punaises

l'araignée les boulons les écrous

la toile d'araignée

le tonneau

la mouche

la hache

le mètre

le marteau

la lime

le pot de peinture

s morceaux de bois

les clous

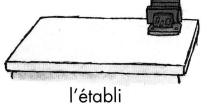
l'établi

les pots

le rabot

11

# La rue

le magasin

le trou

le café

l'ambulance

le trottoir

l'antenne de
télévision

la cheminée

le toit

le bulldozer

l'hôtel

l'autobus

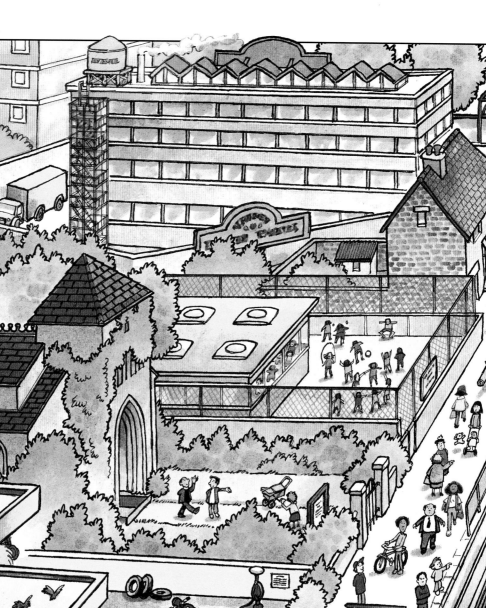

le monsieur

la voiture de
police

les tuyaux

le marteau
piqueur

l'école

la cour de
récréation

le taxi

le passage
pour piétons

l'usine

le camion

le feu
de signalisation

le cinéma

la camionnette

le rouleau
compresseur

la remorque

la maison

le marché

les marches

la moto

bicyclette

le camion de pompiers

l'agent de police

la voiture

la dame

le
lampadaire

l'immeuble

13

# Le magasin de jouets

le train électrique

les dés

la flûte

le robot

les tambours

le collier

l'appareil photo

les perles

les poupées

la guitare

la bague

la maison
de poupée

l'harmonic...

le sifflet

les cubes

le château fort

le sous-marin

la trompette

les flèch...

14

l'arc

le parachute

le bateau
à voiles

les bâtons de
maquillage

le rouleau
compresseur

les masques

la voiture
de course

le cheval à bascule

la tirelire

les billes

les marionnettes

le piano

les astronautes

la grue

la pâte à modeler

le fusil

les soldats
de plomb

la boîte de
peinture

la fusée

15

les balançoires

le bac à sable

le pique-nique

le cerf-volant

la glace

le chien

la barrière

le chemin

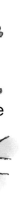

la grenouille

# Le jardin public

le banc

le toboggan

les têtards

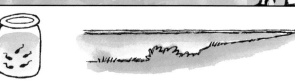

le lac

les rollers

le buisso

bébé · la planche à roulettes · la terre · la poussette · la balançoire

les enfants

le tricycle

les oiseaux

la clôture

le ballon

le bateau

la ficelle

la flaque d'eau

les canetons

la corde à sauter

les arbres

la plate-bande · les cygnes · la laisse · les canards

17

# Le zoo

le panda

l'aile

l'aigle

l'hippopotame

la chauve-souris

le gorille

les pattes

le kangourou

le singe

la queue

le loup

le crocodile

le manchot

l'ours

les plumes

le pélican

l'autruche

le dauphin

la girafe

le lion

les lionceaux

les bois

le cerf

le dromadaire

le phoque

la tortue

l'ours blanc

la trompe

le rhinocéros

le bison

l'éléphant

le castor

la chèvre

le zèbre

le serpent

le requin

la baleine

le tigre

le léopard

# Le voyage

les rails

la locomotive

les tampons

les wagons

le mécanicien

le train de
marchandises

le quai

la contrôleuse

la valise

la billetterie

l'hélicoptère

## La gare

## Le garage

les feux
de signalisation

le sac à dos

les phares

le moteur

la roue

la batterie

20

l'avion

l'hôtesse de l'air

la piste

la tour de contrôle

le steward

le pilote

le lavage-auto

le coffre

l'essence

la dépanneuse

la pompe à essence

aéroport

lavage-auto

camion-citerne

la clef

le pneu

le capot

l'huile

# La campagne

l'éolienne

la montgolfière

le papillon

le lézard

les pierres

le renard

le ruisseau

le poteau
indicateur

le hérisson

l'écluse

la montagne

l'écureuil

la forêt

le blaireau

la rivière

la route

les tentes

le canal

les rondins

le village

le papillon de nuit

le pont

la péniche

la cascade

le hibou

le tunnel

les renardeaux

la taupe

le pêcheur

les rochers

le crapaud

le train

la caravane

la colline

la meule de foin

le chien
de berger

les canards

les agneaux

la mare

les poussins

le grenier

la porcherie

le taureau

les canetons

le poulailler

le tracteur

# La ferme

le coq

les oies

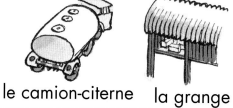

le camion-citerne

la grange

la boue

la
charrette

le fermier

le champ

les poules

le veau

la palissade

la selle

l'étable

la vache

la charrue

le verger

l'écurie

les petits cochons

la bergère

les dindons

l'épouvantail

la vache

le foin

les moutons

les bottes de paille

le cheval

les cochons

la ferme

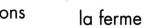

le bateau à voiles

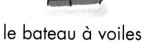
la mer

la rame

le phare

la pelle

le seau

l'étoile de mer

le château
de sable

le parasol

le drapeau

le marin

# La plage

le coquilla

le crabe

la mouette

l'île

le canot à moteur

le ski nautiqu

s vagues

le chapeau de paille

la falaise

le navire

le kayak

la corde

les galets

les algues

le filet

la pagaie

le bateau de pêche

les palmes

l'âne

le poisson

le transat

maillot de bain

le pétrolier

la plage

la barque

27

les ciseaux

le calcul

la gomme

la règle

les photos

les feutres

les punaises

la boîte de peinture

le garçon

le crayon

# L'école

le tableau

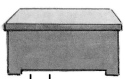

le bureau

les livres

le stylo
à encre

la colle

la craie

le dessi

la corbeille
à papier

l'institutrice

la boîte

la carte

le pinceau

le plafond

le mur

le plancher

a b c d e f g
h i j k l m n
o p q r s t u
v w x y z

le cahier

a b c d e f g
h i j k l m n
o p q r s t u
v w x y z

l'alphabet

le badge

l'aquarium

le papier

le store

le tableau noir

poignée

la plante

la mappemonde

la fille

les crayons cire

la lampe

29

# L'hôpital

l'infirmier

le coton

le médicament

l'ascenseur

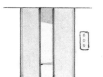
la robe
de chambre

les béquilles

les comprimés

le plateau

la montre

le thermomètre

le rideau

l'ours en peluche

la pomm

le plâtre

la bande

le fauteuil
roulant

le puzzle

le docteur

la seringu

30

# e docteur

les pantoufles

l'ordinateur

le pansement

la banane

le raisin

le panier

les jouets

la poire

les cartes

la couche

la canne

télévision

la chemise
de nuit

le pyjama

l'orange

les mouchoirs
en papier

la BD

la salle d'attente

31

# La fête

le ballon

le chocolat

le bonbon

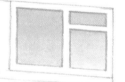

la fenêtre

les feux d'artifice

le ruban

le gâteau

les cadeaux

la paille    la bougie

la guirlande

les jouets

la clémentine

le saucisson

la cassette

la saucisse

les chips

les déguisements

la cerise

le jus de fruits

la framboise

la fraise

l'ampoule

sandwich

le beurre

le biscuit

le fromage

le pain

la nappe

33

# Le magasin

le pamplemousse

la carotte

le chou-fleur

le poireau

le champignon

le concombre

le citron

le céleri

l'abricot

le melon

le sac

FROMAGE

FRUITS ET LÉGUMES

l'oignon

le chou

la pêche

la laitue

les petits pois

la toma

es oeufs

 la prune

 la farine

 la balance

 les bocaux

 la viande

 l'ananas

 le yaourt

 le panier

 les bouteilles

 le sac à main

 le porte-monnaie

 l'argent

les boîtes
de conserve

 le caddie

 es pommes
de terre

les épinards

les haricots

 la caisse

 la citrouille

35

# La nourriture

le déjeuner

le petit déjeuner

l'oeuf à
la coque

le pain grillé

la confiture

le café

l'oeuf au plat

la crème

le lait

les céréales

le chocolat chau

le sucre

le miel

le sel

le poivre

le thé

les crêpes

les petits pains

le dîner

le jambon

la soupe

l'omelette

la salade

les baguettes

le hamburger

le poulet

le riz

le ketchup

les spaghetti

la purée

la pizza

les frites

les desserts

37

# Moi

la tête

les cheveux

la figure

le bras

le coude

le ventre

les doigts de pied

le pied

la jambe

le genou

le sourcil

l'oeil

le nez

la joue

la bouche

les lèvres

les dents

la langue

le menton

les oreilles

le cou

les épaules

la poitrine

le dos

le derrière

la main

le pouce

les doigts

# es vêtements

 chaussettes

 le slip

 le maillot de corps

 le pantalon

 le jean

 le tee-shirt

 la jupe

 la chemise

 la cravate

 le short

 le collant

 la robe

 le pull-over

 le sweat-shirt

 le gilet

 l'écharpe

 le mouchoir

 les tennis

 les chaussures

 les sandales

 les bottes

 les gants

 les poches

 la ceinture

 la boucle

 la fermeture éclair

 le lacet

 le bouton

 les boutonnières

 le manteau

 le blouson

 la casquette

 le chapeau

39

# Les gens

l'acteur

l'actrice

le cuisinier

le danseur

la danseuse

le chanteur

la chanteuse

l'astronaute

le boucher

les agents de police

le menuisier

le pompier

l'artiste

le juge

le mécanicien

la mécanicienne

le coiffeur

le chauffeur de
camion

le conducteur
d'autobus

le serveur
la serveuse

le facteur

la dentiste

l'homme-grenouille

le peintre

la
boulangère

# La famille

le fils
le frère

la fille
la soeur

la mère
la femme

le père
le mari

la tante    l'oncle

le cousin

le grand-père

la grand-mère

# Les actions

sourire

pleurer

penser

écouter

rire

attraper

lancer

casser

peindre

écrire

couper

couper

manger

parler

creuser

porter

boire

faire

sauter

danser

se laver

tricoter

ramper

jouer

regarder

grimper

se bagarrer

dormir

prendre

sauter à
la corde

coudre

attendre

faire la cuisine

se cacher

lire

acheter

pousser

balayer

chanter

cueillir

souffler

tirer

tomber

marcher

courir

être assis

# Les contraires

loin

près

bien

mal

froid

chaud

mouillé

sec

le haut

le bas

sur

sous

sale

propre

gros

maigre

ouvert

fermé

petit

grand

peu

beaucoup

premier

dernier

à gauche

44

dehors

dedans

facile

difficile

vide

plein

mou

dur

devant

haut

lent

rapide

derrière

bas

long

court

mort

vivant

sombre

clair

en haut

vieux

à droite

neuf

en bas

45

# Les jours

lundi

mardi

mercredi

jeudi

vendredi

samedi

dimanche

le calendrie

le matin

le soleil

le soir

la nuit

l'espace

la planète

le vaisseau spatial

la lune

l'étoile

le télescope

46

ours de fête

nniversaire

le cadeau

la bougie

la carte
d'anniversaire

le gâteau d'anniversaire

les vacances

jour du mariage

la demoiselle
d'honneur

la mariée   le marié

l'appareil photo

le photographe

oël

le renne

le père Noël

le traîneau

le sapin de Noël

47

# Le temps

le soleil

les nuage

le ciel

le parapluie

la pluie

l'éclair

le brouillard

la neige

la rosée

le vent

la brume

le givre

l'arc-en-ciel

# Les saisons

le printemps

l'été

l'automne

l'hiver

# es animaux amiliers

le hamster

le cochon d'Inde

perroquet

le bec

la vétérinaire

la niche

le chien

le chiot

la nourriture

la perruche

le lapin

le canari

la cage

le chat     le panier

la souris     le chaton

le lait

les poissons rouges

49

# Les sports

le basket

l'aviron

la voile

la planche à voile

le surf de neige

la raquette

le tennis

le football
américain

la gymnastique

le cricket

le karaté

la balle

la bat

la canne
à pêche

la pêche

l'appât

le rugby

la danse

le base-ball

le plongeon

la piscine

la natation

la course

le tir à l'arc

la cible

le deltaplane

le jogging

le casque

le cyclisme

l'escalade

le judo

le cheval

le poney

le placard

le football

l'équitation

le vestiaire

badminton

les patins à glace

le tennis de table

le patinage

le bâton

le télésiège

les skis

le ski

le sumo

51

# Les couleurs

orange

vert

noir

gris

rouge

marron

rose

blanc

bleu

violet

jaune

# Les formes

le rectangle

le cercle

le losange

le cône

l'étoile

le cube

l'ovale

le triangle

le carré

le croissant

52

# es nombres

| | |
|---|---|
| 1 | un |
| 2 | deux |
| 3 | trois |
| 4 | quatre |
| 5 | cinq |
| 6 | six |
| 7 | sept |
| 8 | huit |
| 9 | neuf |
| 10 | dix |
| 11 | onze |
| 12 | douze |
| 13 | treize |
| 14 | quatorze |
| 15 | quinze |
| 16 | seize |
| 17 | dix-sept |
| 18 | dix-huit |
| 19 | dix-neuf |
| 20 | vingt |

# La fête foraine

le manège

le paillasson

le toboggan géant

la grande roue

le train fantôme

le pop-corn

les anneaux

les montagnes russes

le tir à la carabine

les autos tamponneuses

la barbe à papa

# e cirque

le funambule

la perche

le trapèze

le fil

e cycliste acrobate

l'échelle de corde

le filet

le lapin

les acrobates

le dresseur

le chien

le haut-de-forme

le cerceau

le jongleur

le noeud papillon

l'écuyère

l'orchestre

le clown

# Word list

In this list, you can find all the French words in this book. They are listed in alphabetical order. Next to each one, you can see its pronunciation (how to say it) in letters *like this*, and then its English translation.

Remember that French nouns (words for things) are either masculine or feminine (see page 3). In the list, each one has **le**, **la**, **l'** or **les** in front of it. These all mean "the". The words with **le** are masculine, those with **la** are feminine.

French nouns that begin with "a", "e", "i", "o" or "u", and many that begin with an "h", have **l'** in front of them. At the end, you will see **(m)** or **(f)** to show if the word is masculine or feminine. Plural nouns (a noun is plural if you are talking about more than one, for example "cats") have **les** in front. These are also followed by **(m)** or **(f)**.

## About French pronunciation

Read the pronunciation as if it were an English word, but try to remember the following points about how French words are said:

the French **j** is said like the "s" in "treasure";

when you see *(n)* or *(m)* in a pronunciation, you should barely say the "n" or "m"; say the letter that is before it through your nose, as if you had a cold;

the French **r** is made at the back of the throat and sounds a little like gargling;

the French **u** is not like any sound in English. It is a little like a cross between the "ew" of "few" and the "oo" of "food". To say it, round your lips to say "oo", then try to say "ee"; the pronunciations use the letters "ew" to show this sound.

## A

| | | |
|---|---|---|
| l'abeille (f) | *labbay* | bee |
| l'abricot (m) | *labreeko* | apricot |
| acheter | *a-shuh-tai* | to buy |
| l'acrobate (m/f) | *la-kro-bat* | acrobat (man/ woman) |
| l'acteur (m) | *lak-ter* | actor |
| l'action (f) | *lak-see-o(n)* | action |
| l'actrice (f) | *lak-treess* | actress |
| l'aéroport (m) | *la-ai-roppor* | airport |
| l'agent de police (m) | *la-jo(n) duh poleess* | policeman |
| l'agneau (m) | *lan-yo* | lamb |
| l'aigle (m) | *laigl* | eagle |
| l'aile (f) | *lail* | wing |
| les algues (f) | *lez alg* | seaweed |
| les allumettes (f) | *lez allewmett* | matches |
| l'alphabet (m) | *lalfa-bai* | alphabet |
| l'ambulance (f) | *lo(m)bewla(n)ss* | ambulance |
| l'ampoule (f) | *lo(m)pool* | bulb (light) |
| l'animal familier (m) | *lanneemal fammeel-yai* | pet |
| l'ananas (m) | *la-na-na* | pineapple |
| l'âne (m) | *lan* | donkey |
| les anneaux (m) | *lez annaw* | ring toss |
| l'anniversaire (m) | *lannee-vair-sair* | birthday |
| l'antenne de télévision (f) | *lo(n)tenn duh tailaiveez-yo(n)* | TV antenna |
| l'appareil photo (m) | *lappa-ray fotto* | camera |
| l'appât (m) | *lappa* | bait |
| l'appentis (m) | *la-po(n)tee* | shed |
| l'aquarium (m) | *lakwaree-om* | aquarium |
| l'araignée (f) | *la-renn-yai* | spider |
| l'arbre (m) | *lar-br* | tree |
| l'arc (m) | *lar-k* | bow |
| l'arc-en-ciel (m) | *lar-ko(n)-see-el* | rainbow |
| l'argent (m) | *lar-jo(n)* | money |
| l'armoire (f) | *lar-mwar* | armoire |

| | | |
|---|---|---|
| l'arrosoir (m) | *la-rozwar* | watering can |
| l'artiste (m/f) | *lar-teest* | artist (man/woman) |
| l'ascenseur (m) | *lasso(n)-ser* | elevator |
| l'aspirateur (m) | *lass-peera-ter* | vacuum cleaner |
| l'assiette (f) | *lassee-yet* | plate |
| l'astronaute (m/f) | *lass-tronnawt* | spaceman/woman |
| l'atelier (m) | *lattuh-lee-yai* | workshop |
| attendre | *atto(n)dr* | to wait |
| attraper | *attra-pai* | to catch |
| l'autobus (m) | *lotto-bewss* | bus |
| l'automne (m) | *lo-tonn* | autumn |
| les autos tamponneuses (f) | *lez otto to(m)ponnerz* | bumper cars |
| l'autruche (f) | *law-trewsh* | ostrich |
| l'avion (m) | *lav-yo(n)* | plane |

## B

| | | |
|---|---|---|
| le bac à sable | *luh bak-assabl* | sandbox |
| le badge | *luh badj* | badge |
| le badminton | *luh bad-meen-ton* | badminton |
| la bague | *la bag* | ring |
| les baguettes (f) | *lai baggett* | chopsticks |
| la baignoire | *la bai-nwar* | bathtub |
| le balai | *luh ballai* | broom |
| le balai à franges | *luh ballai-a-fro(n)j* | mop |
| la balance | *la ballo(n)ss* | scales |
| la balançoire | *la ballo(n)-swar* | seesaw |
| les balançoires (f) | *lai ballo(n)-swar* | swings |
| balayer | *ballai-yai* | to sweep |
| la baleine | *la ballenn* | whale |
| la balle | *la bal* | ball (small) |
| le ballon | *luh ballo(n)* | ball (large), balloon |
| la banane | *la bannan* | banana |
| le banc | *luh bo(n)* | bench |
| la bande | *la bon(n)d* | bandage |
| la barbe à papa | *la bar-ba pappa* | cotton candy |
| la barque | *la bar-rk* | rowboat |
| la barrière | *la bar-yair* | gate |

| French | Pronunciation | English |
|---|---|---|
| as | luh ba | low |
| ...ase-ball | luh baiz-boll | bottom (not top) |
| ...asket | luh bass-ket | baseball |
| ...ateau | luh battaw | basketball |
| ...ateau à voiles | luh battaw a vwal | boat |
| ...ateau de pêche | luh battaw duh paish | sailboat |
| ...âton | luh batto(n) | fishing boat |
| ...âton (de ski) | luh batto(n) (duh skee) | stick |
| ...âtons de | lai batto(n) duh | ski pole |
| ...aquillage (m) | makee-yaj | facepaints |
| ...atte | la bat | bat |
| ...atterie | la bat-ree | battery |
| ...D | la bai-dai | comic book |
| ...aucoup | baw-koo | many |
| ...ébé | luh baibai | baby |
| ...ec | luh bek | beak |
| ...êche | la baish | shovel |
| ...béquilles (f) | lai bekee-yuh | crutches |
| ...berger | luh bair-jai | shepherd |
| ...ergère | la bair-jair | shepherdess |
| ...eurre | luh burr | butter |
| ...bicyclette | la bee-seeklett | bicycle |
| ...n | bee-ya(n) | good |
| ...billes (f) | lai bee-yuh | marbles |
| ...oilletterie | la bee-yet-uhree | ticket machine |
| ...oinette | la beennet | hoe |
| ...biscuit | luh beess-kwee | cookie |
| ...oison | luh beezo(n) | bison |
| ...olaireau | luh blai-raw | badger |
| ...anc | blo(n) | white |
| ...u | bluh | blue |
| ...olouson | luh bloo-zo(n) | jacket |
| ...bocaux (m) | lai bokkaw | jars |
| ...ire | bwar | to drink |
| ...bois | luh bwa | wood |
| ...boîte | la bwatt | box |
| ...boîte à outils | la bwa-ta-ootee | toolbox |
| ...boîte de conserve | la bwatt duh ko(n)sairv | can (of food) |
| ...boîte de peinture | la bwatt duh pa(n)tewr | paintbox |
| ...bol | luh bol | bowl |
| ...bonbon | luh bo(n)bo(n) | candy |
| ...botte | la bot | boot (to wear) |
| ...botte de paille | la bot duh pie | straw bale |
| ...bouche | la boosh | mouth |
| ...boucher | luh booshai | butcher (man) |
| ...bouchère | la booshair | butcher (woman) |
| ...boucle | la bookl | buckle |
| ...boue | la boo | mud |
| ...bougie | la boo-jee | candle |
| ...bouilloire | la booy-war | kettle |
| ...boulanger | luh boolo(n)-jai | baker (man) |
| ...boulangère | la boolo(n)-jair | baker (woman) |
| ...boulon | luh boolo(n) | bolt |
| ...bouteille | la boo-tay | bottle |
| ...bouton | luh booto(n) | button |
| ...boutonnières (f) | lai boo-ton-yair | button holes |
| ...bras | luh bra | arm |
| ...brique | la breek | brick |
| ...brosse | la bross | brush |
| ...brosse à cheveux | la brossa-shuh-vuh | hairbrush |
| ...brosse à dents | la brossa-do(n) | toothbrush |
| ...brouette | la broo-ett | wheelbarrow |

| French | Pronunciation | English |
|---|---|---|
| le brouillard | luh broo-yar | fog |
| la brume | la brewm | mist |
| le buisson | luh bwee-so(n) | bush |
| le bulldozer | luh bewl-daw-zair | bulldozer |
| le bureau | luh bew-raw | desk |

## C

| French | Pronunciation | English |
|---|---|---|
| le caddie | luh kaddee | trolley |
| le cadeau | luh kaddaw | present (gift) |
| le café | luh kaffai | café, coffee |
| la cage | la kaj | cage |
| le cahier | luh ka-yai | notebook |
| la caisse | la kess | checkout |
| le calcul | luh kal-kewl | problems |
| le calendrier | luh kallo(n)-dree-yai | calendar |
| le camion | luh kam-yo(n) | truck |
| le camion de pompiers | luh kam-yo(n) duh po(m)p-yai | fire engine |
| le camion-citerne | luh kam-yo(n) seetairn | tanker (truck) |
| la camionnette | la kam-yonnett | van |
| la campagne | la ko(m)-pan-yuh | countryside |
| le canal | luh kannal | canal |
| le canapé | luh kannapai | sofa |
| le canard | luh kannar | duck |
| le canari | luh kannaree | canary |
| le caneton | luh kan-to(n) | duckling |
| le canif | luh kanneef | penknife |
| la canne | la kan | walking stick |
| la canne à pêche | la kanna pesh | fishing rod |
| le canot à moteur | luh kannaw-a-motter | motorboat |
| le capot | luk kappo | hood (car) |
| la caravane | la ka-ra-van | camper |
| la carotte | ka-rot | carrot |
| le carré | luh karrai | square |
| les carreaux (m) | lai karro | tiles |
| la carte | la kar-t | card, map |
| la carte d'anniversaire | la kar-t dannee-vair-sair | birthday card |
| la cascade | la kass-kad | waterfall |
| le casque | luh kask | helmet |
| la casquette | la kass-ket | cap |
| casser | kassai | to break |
| la casserole | la kass-rol | saucepan |
| la cassette | la kassett | cassette |
| la cassette vidéo | la kassett veedai-o | video (cassette) |
| le castor | luh kass-tor | beaver |
| le CD | luh sai-dai | CD (compact disc) |
| la ceinture | la sa(n)tewr | belt |
| le céleri | luh sell-ree | celery |
| le cerceau | luh sair-saw | hoop |
| le cercle | luh sairkl | circle |
| les céréales (f) | lai sai-rai-al | cereal |
| le cerf | luh sair | deer |
| le cerf-volant | luh sair vollo(n) | kite |
| la cerise | la suh-reez | cherry |
| la chaise | la shaiz | chair |
| la chambre | la sho(m)br | bedroom |
| le champ | luh sho(m) | field |
| le champignon | luh sho(m)peen-yo(n) | mushroom |
| chanter | sho(n)tai | to sing |
| le chanteur | luh sho(n)-ter | singer (man) |
| la chanteuse | la sho(n)-terz | singer (woman) |
| le chapeau | luh shappo | hat |
| le chapeau de paille | luh shappo duh pie | straw hat |

| French | Pronunciation | English |
|---|---|---|
| la charrette | la sharrett | cart |
| la charrue | la sharrew | plow |
| le chat | luh sha | cat |
| le château de sable | luh shatto duh sabl | sandcastle |
| le château fort | luh shatto for | castle |
| le chaton | luh shatto(n) | kitten |
| chaud | shaw | hot |
| le chauffeur de camion | luh shoffer duh kam-yo(n) | truck driver (man/woman) |
| la chaussette | la shossett | sock |
| la chaussure | la shossewr | shoe |
| la chauve-souris | la shawv-sooree | bat |
| le chemin | luh shuh-ma(n) | path, lane |
| la cheminée | la shuh-meenai | chimney |
| la chemise | la shuh-meez | shirt |
| la chemise de nuit | la shuh-meez duh nwee | nightgown |
| la chenille | la shuh-nee-yuh | caterpillar |
| le cheval | luh shuh-val | horse |
| le cheval à bascule | luh shuh-val a baskewl | rocking horse |
| les cheveux (m) | lai shuh-vuh | hair |
| la chèvre | la shaivr | goat |
| le chien | luh shee-a(n) | dog |
| le chien de berger | luh shee-a(n) duh bair-jai | sheepdog |
| le chiffon | luh shee-fo(n) | dust cloth |
| le chiot | shee-o | puppy |
| les chips (f) | lai sheeps | chips |
| le chocolat | luh sho-ko-la | chocolate |
| le chocolat chaud | luh sho-ko-la shaw | hot chocolate |
| le chou | luh shoo | cabbage |
| le chou-fleur | luh shoo-fler | cauliflower |
| la cible | la seebl | target |
| le ciel | luh see-ell | sky |
| le cinéma | luh seenaima | movie theater |
| cinq | sank | five |
| le cirque | luh seerk | circus |
| les ciseaux (m) | lai seezaw | scissors |
| le citron | luh seetro(n) | lemon |
| la citrouille | la seetroo-yuh | pumpkin |
| clair | klair | light (not dark) |
| la clé | la klai | key |
| la clef | la klai | wrench |
| la clémentine | la klemmo(n)-teen | tangerine |
| la clôture | la klaw-tewr | fence |
| le clown | luh kloon | clown |
| le clou | luh kloo | nail |
| la coccinelle | la kok-see-nell | ladybug |
| le cochon | luh ko-sho(n) | pig |
| le cochon d'Inde | luh ko-sho(n) da(n)d | guinea pig |
| le coffre | luh kofr | trunk (of car) |
| le coiffeur | luh kwa-fer | barber |
| la coiffeuse | la kwa-ferz | hair stylist (woman) |
| le collant | luh ko-lo(n) | tights |
| la colle | la kol | glue |
| le collier | luh kol-yai | necklace |
| la colline | la kolleen | hill |
| la commode | la ko-mod | chest of drawers |
| le comprimé | luh ko(m)pree-mai | pill |
| le concombre | luh ko(n)-ko(m)br | cucumber |
| le conducteur d'autobus | luh ko(n)-dewkter daw-taw-bewss | bus driver (man) |
| la conductrice d'autobus | la ko(n)-dewktreess daw-taw-bewss | bus driver (woman) |
| le cône | luh kawn | cone |
| la confiture | la ko(n)fee-tewr | jam |
| le contraire | luh ko(n)trair | opposite |
| le contrôleur | luh ko(n)traw-ler | conductor (man) |
| la contrôleuse | la ko(n)traw-lerz | conductor (woman) |
| les copeaux (m) | lai koppaw | (wood) shavings |
| le coq | luh kok | rooster |
| le coquillage | luh ko-kee-yaj | shell |
| la corbeille à papier | la kor-bay a pap-yai | wastepaper basket |
| la corde | la kord | rope |
| la corde à sauter | la kord-a-sawtai | jump rope |
| le coton | luh ko-to(n) | cotton |
| le cou | luh koo | neck |
| la couche | la koosh | diaper |
| le coude | luh kood | elbow |
| coudre | koodr | to sew |
| la couette | la koo-ett | comforter |
| la couleur | la koo-ler | color |
| couper | koo-pai | to cut, to chop |
| la cour de récréation | la koor duh rekrai-ass-yo(n) | playground |
| courir | kooreer | to run |
| la course | la koorss | race |
| court | koor | short |
| le cousin | luh kooza(n) | cousin (boy) |
| la cousine | la koozeen | cousin (girl) |
| le coussin | luh koo-sa(n) | cushion |
| le couteau | luh koo-taw | knife |
| le crabe | luh krab | crab |
| la craie | la krai | chalk |
| le crapaud | luh kra-paw | toad |
| la cravate | la kra-vat | tie |
| le crayon | luh krai-yo(n) | pencil |
| les crayons cire (m) | lai krai-yo(n) seer | crayons |
| la crème | la krem | cream |
| la crêpe | la kraip | pancake |
| creuser | kruh-zai | to dig |
| le cricket | luh kree-ket | cricket (sport) |
| le crocodile | luh kro-ko-deel | crocodile |
| le croissant | luh krwa-so(n) | crescent |
| le cube | luh kewb | cube |
| les cubes (m) | lai kewb | blocks |
| cueillir | kuh-yeer | to pick |
| la cuillère en bois | la kwee-yair o(n) bwa | wooden spoon |
| la cuisine | la kwee-zeen | kitchen |
| le cuisinier | luh kwee-zeen-yai | cook (man) |
| la cuisinière | la kwee-zeen-yair | stove, cook (woman) |
| le cyclisme | luh see-kleessm | cycling |
| le/la cycliste acrobate | luh/la see-kleest akro-bat | unicyclist (man/woman) |
| le cygne | luh seen-yuh | swan |

## D

| French | Pronunciation | English |
|---|---|---|
| la dame | la dam | woman, lady |
| la danse | la do(n)ss | dance |
| danser | do(n)sai | to dance |
| le danseur | luh do(n)-ser | dancer (man) |
| la danseuse | la do(n)-serz | dancer (woman) |
| le dauphin | luh daw-fa(n) | dolphin |
| dedans | duhdo(n) | in, inside |
| les déguisements (m) | lai dai-guee-zuh-mo(n) | costume |
| dehors | duh-or | out, outside |
| le déjeuner | dai-juh-nai | lunch (lunchtime meal) |
| le deltaplane | delta-plan | hang gliding |
| la demoiselle d'honneur | la duh-mwa-zel do-ner | bridesmaid |
| le dentifrice | luh do(n)tee-freess | toothpaste |
| le/la dentiste | luh/la do(n)teest | dentist (man/woman) |
| la dent | la do(n) | tooth |
| la dépanneuse | la depannerz | tow truck |
| le déplantoir | luh deplo(n)-twar | trowel |
| dernier | dairn-yai | last |
| le derrière | luh dair-yair | bottom (of body) |

| | | |
|---|---|---|
| dés (m) | lai dai | dice |
| escente de lit | la desso(n)t duh lee | rug |
| essert | luh dessair | dessert |
| essin | luh dessa(n) | drawing |
| x | duh | two |
| ant | duhvo(n) | front |
| cile | dee-fee-seel | difficult |
| anche | dee-mo(n)sh | Sunday |
| indon | luh da(n)-do(n) | turkey |
| îner | luh deenai | dinner (evening meal) |
| | deess | ten |
| huit | deez-weet | eighteen |
| neuf | deez-nerf | nineteen |
| sept | deesset | seventeen |
| octeur | luh dokter | doctor |
| oigt | luh dwa | finger |
| oigt de pied | luh dwa duh p-yai | toe |
| mir | dor-meer | to sleep |
| os | luh daw | back (of body) |
| ouche | la doosh | shower |
| ze | dooz | twelve |
| rap | luh dra | sheet |
| rapeau | luh dra-paw | flag |
| resseur | luh dress-er | ring master |
| roite | a drwat | (on/to the) right |
| romadaire | luh dromma-dair | camel |
| | dewr | hard |
| | | |
| au (f) | law | water |
| charpe (f) | laisharp | scarf |
| chelle (f) | laishell | ladder |
| chelle de corde (f) | laishell duh kord | rope ladder |
| clair (m) | lai-klair | lightning |
| cluse (f) | lai-klewz | lock (on canal) |
| cole (f) | lai-koll | school |
| outer | aikootai | to listen |
| rire | aikreer | to write |
| crou (m) | laikroo | nut (nuts and bolts) |
| cureuil (m) | laikew-ruh-yuh | squirrel |
| curie (f) | laikew-ree | stable |
| cuyer (m) | laikweeyai | (bareback) rider (man) |
| cuyère (f) | laikweeyair | (bareback) rider (woman) |
| léphant (m) | lailaifo(n) | elephant |
| bas | o(n) ba | downstairs |
| nfant (m/f) | lo(n)fo(n) | child |
| haut | o(n)-aw | upstairs |
| ntrée (f) | lo(n)trai | hall |
| olienne (f) | lai-ol-yen | windmill |
| paule (f) | lai-pawl | shoulder |
| s épinards (m) | lez aipeenar | spinach |
| ponge (f) | laipo(n)j | sponge |
| pouvantail (m) | laipoo-vo(n)-tie | scarecrow |
| quitation (f) | laikeetass-yo(n) | riding |
| scalade (f) | leska-lad | climbing |
| scalier (m) | leskal-yai | stairs, staircase |
| scargot (m) | leskar-gaw | snail |
| space (m) | lespass | space |
| ssence (f) | lesso(n)ss | gasoline |
| table (f) | laita-bl | cowshed |
| tabli (m) | laita-blee | workbench |
| tau (m) | lettaw | vice |
| té (m) | lettai | summer |
| toile (f) | letwal | star |
| toile de mer (f) | letwal duh mair | starfish |

| | | |
|---|---|---|
| être assis | aitr assee | to sit |
| l'évier (m) | lev-yai | sink |

## F

| | | |
|---|---|---|
| facile | fa-seel | easy |
| le facteur | luh fakter | mail carrier (man) |
| la factrice | la faktreess | mail carrier (woman) |
| faire | fair | to make |
| faire la cuisine | fair la kwee-zeen | to cook |
| la falaise | la fa-laiz | cliff |
| la famille | la fa-mee-yuh | family |
| la farine | la fa-reen | flour |
| le fauteuil roulant | luh fawtuh-yuh roolo(n) | wheelchair |
| la femme | la fam | woman, wife |
| la fenêtre | la fuh-naitr | window |
| le fer à repasser | luh faira-ruhpassai | iron |
| la ferme | la fairm | farm, farmhouse |
| fermé | fairmai | closed |
| la fermeture éclair | la fairmuh-tewr eklair | zipper |
| le fermier | luh fairm-yai | farmer (man) |
| la fermière | la fairm-yair | farmer (woman) |
| la fête | la fait | party |
| la fête foraine | la fait forain | fair, fairground |
| le feu | luh fuh | fire |
| le feu de signalisation | luh fuh duh seen-ya-leezasseeo(n) | traffic lights |
| la feuille | la fer-yuh | leaf |
| les feutres (m) | lai fuhtr | felt-tip pens |
| les feux d'artifice (m) | lai fuh da-rteefeess | fireworks |
| les feux de signalisation (m) | lai fuh duh seen-ya-leezasseeo(n) | signals (railway) |
| la ficelle | la fee-sell | string |
| la figure | la fee-gewr | face |
| le fil | luh feel | thread |
| le filet | luh fee-lai | net |
| la fille | la fee-yuh | girl, daughter |
| le fils | luh feess | son |
| la flaque d'eau | la flak daw | puddle |
| la flèche | la flesh | arrow |
| la fleur | la fler | flower |
| la flûte | la flewt | flute |
| le foin | luh fwa(n) | hay |
| le football | luh foot-bol | soccer |
| le football américain | luh foot-bol a-maireeka(n) | football |
| la forêt | la forrai | forest |
| la forme | la form | shape |
| la fourche | la foorsh | pitchfork |
| la fourchette | la foorshett | fork |
| la fraise | la fraiz | strawberry |
| la framboise | la fro(m)-bwaz | raspberry |
| le frère | luh frair | brother |
| les frites (f) | lai freet | fries |
| froid | frwa | cold |
| le fromage | luh frommaj | cheese |
| le fruit | luh frwee | fruit |
| la fumée | la few-mai | smoke |
| le/la funambule | luh/la few-no(m)-bewl | tightrope walker (man/woman) |
| la fusée | la few-zai | rocket |
| le fusil | luh fewzee | gun |

## G

| | | |
|---|---|---|
| le galet | luh gallai | pebble |
| le gant | luh gu(n) | glove |
| le garage | luh ga-raj | garage |
| le garçon | luh gar-so(n) | boy |

| | | |
|---|---|---|
| la gare | *la gar* | station |
| le gâteau | *luh ga-taw* | cake |
| le gâteau d'anniversaire | *luh ga-taw dannee-vair-sair* | birthday cake |
| à gauche | *a gawsh* | (on/to) the left |
| le genou | *luh juh-noo* | knee |
| les gens (m/f) | *lai jo(n)* | people |
| le gilet | *luh jee-lai* | cardigan |
| la girafe | *la jee-raf* | giraffe |
| le givre | *luh jeevr* | frost |
| la glace | *la glahss* | ice cream |
| la gomme | *la gom* | eraser |
| le gorille | *luh goree-yuh* | gorilla |
| la graine | *la grenn* | seed |
| grand | *gro(n)* | big |
| la grand-mère | *la gro(n)-mair* | grandmother |
| le grand-père | *luh gro(n) pair* | grandfather |
| la grande roue | *la gro(n)d roo* | Ferris wheel |
| la grange | *la gro(n)j* | barn |
| le grenier | *luh gruhn-yai* | attic |
| la grenouille | *la gruh-noo-yuh* | frog |
| grimper | *gra(m)pai* | to climb |
| gris | *gree* | grey |
| gros | *graw* | fat |
| la grue | *la grew* | crane |
| la guêpe | *la gaip* | wasp |
| la guirlande | *la geer-lo(n)d* | paper chains |
| la guitare | *la gee-tarr* | guitar |
| la gymnastique | *la jeem-nasteek* | gym |

## H

| | | |
|---|---|---|
| la hache | *la ash* | axe |
| la haie | *la ai* | hedge |
| le hamburger | *luh a(m)boor-ger* | hamburger |
| le hamster | *luh am-stair* | hamster |
| le haricot | *luh aree-kaw* | bean |
| l'harmonica (m) | *larmoneeka* | harmonica |
| haut | *aw* | high |
| le haut | *luh aw* | top |
| le haut-de-forme | *!uh aw duh form* | top hat |
| l'hélicoptère (m) | *lellee-koptair* | helicopter |
| l'herbe (f) | *lairb* | grass |
| le hérisson | *luh airee-so(n)* | hedgehog |
| le hibou | *luh eeboo* | owl |
| l'hippopotame (m) | *leepo-pottam* | hippopotamus |
| l'hiver (m) | *lee-vair* | winter |
| l'homme-grenouille (m) | *lom gruhnoo-yuh* | frogman |
| l'hôpital (m) | *law-peetal* | hospital |
| l'hôtel (m) | *law-tell* | hotel |
| l'hôtesse de l'air (f) | *lawtess duh lair* | flight attendant |
| l'huile (f) | *lweel* | oil |
| huit | *weet* | eight |

## I

| | | |
|---|---|---|
| l'île (f) | *leel* | island |
| l'immeuble (m) | *lee-merbl* | apartment building |
| l'infirmier (m) | *la(n)feerm-yai* | nurse (man) |
| l'infirmière (f) | *la(n)feerm-yair* | nurse (woman) |
| l'instituteur (m) | *la(n)stee-tewter* | teacher (man) |
| l'institutrice (f) | *la(n)stee-tewtreess* | teacher (woman) |
| l'interrupteur (m) | *la(n)terrewp-ter* | switch |

## J

| | | |
|---|---|---|
| la jambe | *la jo(m)b* | leg |
| le jambon | *luh jo(m)bo(n)* | ham |
| le jardin | *luh jarda(n)* | garden |
| le jardin public | *luh jarda(n) pewbleek* | park |
| jaune | *jawn* | yellow |
| le jean | *luh djeen* | jeans |
| jeudi | *juhdee* | Thursday |
| le jogging | *luh djogeeng* | jogging |
| le jongleur | *luh jo(n)gl-er* | juggler (man) |
| la jongleuse | *la jo(n)glerz* | juggler (woman) |
| la joue | *la joo* | cheek |
| jouer | *joo-ai* | to play |
| le jouet | *luh joo-ai* | toy |
| le journal | *luh joor-nal* | newspaper |
| le jour | *le joor* | day |
| le jour de fête | *luh joor duh fait* | (public) holiday, festival |
| le jour du mariage | *luh joor dew marree-aj* | wedding day |
| le judo | *luh jew-daw* | judo |
| le juge | *luh jewj* | judge (man/ woman) |
| la jupe | *la jewp* | skirt |
| le jus de fruits | *luh jew duh frwee* | fruit juice |

## K

| | | |
|---|---|---|
| le kangourou | *luh ko(n)-gooroo* | kangaroo |
| le karaté | *luh karatai* | karate |
| le kayak | *luh kayak* | kayak |
| le ketchup | *luh ketchup* | ketchup |

## L

| | | |
|---|---|---|
| le lac | *luh lak* | lake |
| le lacet | *luh lassai* | shoelace |
| la laisse | *la less* | lead |
| le lait | *luh lai* | milk |
| la laitue | *la laitew* | lettuce |
| le lampadaire | *luh lo(m)pa-dair* | street light |
| la lampe | *la lo(m)p* | lamp |
| lancer | *lo(n)sai* | to throw |
| le landau | *luh lo(n)daw* | baby buggy |
| la langue | *la lo(n)g* | tongue |
| le lapin | *luh la-pa(n)* | rabbit |
| le lavabo | *luh la-vabbaw* | sink |
| le lavage-auto | *luh la-vaj-otto* | car wash |
| le lave-linge | *luh lav-la(n)j* | washing machine |
| le légume | *luh legewm* | vegetable |
| lent | *lo(n)* | slow |
| le léopard | *luh lai-opar* | leopard |
| la lettre | *la letr* | letter |
| la lèvre | *la laivr* | lip |
| le lézard | *luh lezar* | lizard |
| la lime | *la leem* | file |
| le lion | *luh lee-o(n)* | lion |
| le lionceau | *luh lee-o(n)saw* | lion cub |
| lire | *leer* | to read |
| le lit | *luh lee* | bed |
| le livre | *luh leevr* | book |
| la locomotive | *la lo-ko-moteev* | (train) engine |
| loin | *lwa(n)* | far |
| long | *lo(n)* | long |
| le losange | *luh lo-zo(n)j* | diamond |
| le loup | *luh loo* | wolf |
| lundi | *lu(n)dee* | Monday |
| la lune | *la lewn* | moon |

## M

| | | |
|---|---|---|
| le magasin | *luh magga-za(n)* | shop |
| le magasin de jouets | *luh magga-za(n) duh joo-ai* | toyshop |
| maigre | *maigr* | thin |

| French | Pronunciation | English |
|---|---|---|
| aillot de bain | luh ma-yo duh ba(n) | swimsuit |
| aillot de corps | luh ma-yo duh kor | undershirt |
| ain | la ma(n) | hand |
| aison | la mai-zo(n) | house |
| aison de poupée | la mai-zo(n) duh poopai | doll's house |
| mal | | bad |
| anchot | luh mo(n)-shaw | penguin |
| anège | luh man-aij | merry-go-round |
| ger | mo(n)jai | to eat |
| anteau | luh mo(n)taw | coat |
| appemonde | la map-mo(n)d | globe |
| arché | luh mar-shai | market |
| cher | mar-shai | to walk |
| arche | la ma-rsh | step |
| are | la mar | pond |
| di | mar-dee | Tuesday |
| ari | luh ma-ree | husband |
| arié | luh ma-ree-ai | bridegroom |
| ariée | la ma-ree-ai | bride |
| arin | luh ma-ra(n) | sailor |
| arionnette | la ma-ree-onett | puppet |
| ron | ma-ro(n) | brown |
| arteau | luh ma-rtaw | hammer |
| arteau piqueur | luh ma-rtaw pee-ker | drill |
| asque | luh ma-sk | mask |
| atin | luh ma-ta(n) | morning |
| écanicien | luh mekka-neess-ya(n) | mechanic, train driver (man) |
| écanicienne | la mekka-neess-yen | mechanic, train driver (woman) |
| édicament | luh meddee-kahmo(n) | medicine |
| elon | luh muhlo(n) | melon |
| enton | luh mo(n)to(n) | chin |
| enuisier | luh muhn-weez-yai | carpenter |
| er | la mair | sea |
| rcredi | mair-kruh-dee | Wednesday |
| ère | la mair | mother |
| ètre | luh maitr | tape measure |
| eule de foin | la merl duh fwa(n) | haystack |
| iel | luh mee-ell | honey |
| iroir | luh meer-wahr | mirror |
| i | mwa | me |
| onsieur | luh muhss-yuh | man |
| ontagne | la mo(n)-tan-yuh | mountain |
| montagnes russes (f) | lai mo(n)-tan-yuh rewss | roller coaster |
| ontgolfière | la mo(n)golf-yair | hot-air balloon |
| ontre | la mo(n)tr | watch |
| oquette | la mo-kett | carpet |
| orceau de bois | luh mor-saw duh bwa | wood |
| rt | mor | dead |
| oteur | maw-ter | engine |
| oto | la mawtaw | motorcycle |
| ou | moo | soft |
| ouche | la moosh | fly |
| ouchoir | luh moosh-wahr | handkerchief |
| ouchoir en papier | luh moosh-wahr o(n) pap-yai | tissue |
| uillé | moo-yai | wet |
| ouette | la moo-ett | seagull |
| outon | luh moo-to(n) | sheep |
| ur | luh mewr | wall |
| nappe | la nap | tablecloth |
| natation | la na-tass-yo(n) | swimming |
| navire | luh na-veer | ship |
| neige | la naij | snow |
| uf | nerf | new, nine |

| French | Pronunciation | English |
|---|---|---|
| le nez | luh nai | nose |
| la niche | la neesh | kennel |
| le nid | luh nee | nest |
| Noël | no-ell | Christmas |
| le noeud papillon | luh nuh papee-yo(n) | bow tie |
| noir | nwar | black |
| le nombre | luh no(m)br | number |
| la nourriture | la nooree-tewr | food |
| le nuage | luh new-aj | cloud |
| la nuit | la nwee | night |

## O

| French | Pronunciation | English |
|---|---|---|
| l'oeil (m) | ler-yuh | eye |
| l'oeuf (m) | lerf | egg |
| l'oeuf à la coque (m) | lerf-alla-kok | boiled egg |
| l'oeuf au plat (m) | lerf-awpla | fried egg |
| l'oie (f) | lwa | goose |
| l'oignon (m) | lonn-yo(n) | onion |
| l'oiseau (m) | lwa-zaw | bird |
| l'omelette (f) | lom-let | omelette |
| l'oncle (m) | lo(n)kl | uncle |
| onze | o(n)z | eleven |
| orange | oro(n)j | orange (color) |
| l'orange (f) | oro(n)j | orange (fruit) |
| l'orchestre (m) | lor-kestr | orchestra |
| l'ordinateur (m) | lordee-na-ter | computer |
| les ordures (f) | lez ordewr | garbage |
| l'oreille (f) | lo-ray | ear |
| l'oreiller (m) | lorai-yai | pillow |
| l'os (m) | loss | bone |
| l'ours (m) | loorss | bear |
| l'ours blanc (m) | loorss blo(n) | polar bear |
| l'ours en peluche (m) | loorss o(n) plewsh | teddy bear |
| ouvert | oovair | open |
| l'ovale (m) | lo-val | oval |

## P

| French | Pronunciation | English |
|---|---|---|
| la pagaie | la paggai | paddle |
| la paille | la pie | (drinking) straw |
| le pain | luh pa(n) | bread |
| le pain grillé | luh pa(n) gree-yai | toast |
| le paillasson | luh pie-ya-so(n) | mat |
| la palissade | la pallee-sad | fence |
| les palmes (f) | lai palm | flippers |
| le pamplemousse | luh po(m)pl-mooss | grapefruit |
| le panda | luh po(n)-da | panda |
| le panier | luh pan-yai | basket |
| le pansement | luh po(n)s-mo(n) | bandage |
| le pantalon | luh po(n)-ta-lo(n) | pants |
| la pantoufle | lai po(n)toofl | slipper |
| le papier | luh pap-yai | paper |
| le papier de verre | luh pap-yai duh vair | sandpaper |
| le papier hygiénique | luh pap-yai ee-jyaineek | toilet paper |
| le papillon | luh pa-pee-yo(n) | butterfly |
| le papillon de nuit | luh pa-pee-yo(n) duh nwee | moth |
| le paquet de lessive | luh pa-kai duh lesseev | laundry detergent |
| le parachute | luh pa-ra-shewt | parachute |
| le parapluie | luh pa-ra-plwee | umbrella |
| le parasol | luh pa-ra-sol | beach umbrella |
| parler | pa-rlai | to talk |
| le passage pour piétons | luh pa-saj poor pee-ai-to(n) | crosswalk |
| la pâte à modeler | la pat a mo-duh-lai | playdough |
| le patinage | luh pa-tee-nahj | ice skating |
| le patin à glace | luh pa-ta(n) a glas | ice skate |
| la patte | la pat | paw |
| la pêche | la paish | fishing |

| | | |
|---|---|---|
| le pêcheur | *luh pesh-er* | fisherman |
| le peigne | *luh penn-yuh* | comb |
| peindre | *pa(n)dr* | to paint |
| le peintre | *luh pa(n)tr* | painter |
| le pélican | *luh pelleeko(n)* | pelican |
| la pelle | *la pell* | shovel |
| la pelle à ordures | *la pell a ordewr* | dustpan |
| la pendule | *la po(n)dewl* | clock |
| la péniche | *la penneesh* | barge |
| penser | *po(n)sai* | to think |
| la perceuse | *la pair-suhz* | drill |
| le père | *luh pair* | father |
| le père Noël | *luh pair no-ell* | Santa Claus |
| la perle | *la perl* | bead |
| le perroquet | *luh perrokai* | parrot |
| la perruche | *la perrewsh* | parakeet |
| petit | *puh-tee* | small |
| le petit déjeuner | *luh puh-tee dai-juh-nai* | breakfast |
| la petite cuillère | *la puh-teet kwee-yair* | teaspoon |
| le petit cochon | *luh puhtee kosho(n)* | piglet |
| le petit pain | *luh puhtee pa(n)* | bread roll |
| les petits pois (m) | *lai puh-tee pwa* | peas |
| le pétrolier | *luh petrol-yai* | oil tanker (ship) |
| peu | *puh* | few |
| le phare | *luh fahr* | lighthouse |
| les phares (m) | *lai fahr* | headlights |
| le phoque | *luh fok* | seal |
| la photo | *la fottaw* | photograph |
| le/la photographe | *luh/la fottaw-graf* | photographer (man /woman) |
| le piano | *luh pee-anno* | piano |
| le pied | *luh pee-ai* | foot |
| la pierre | *la pee-air* | stone |
| le pigeon | *luh pee-jo(n)* | pigeon |
| le pilote | *luh pee-lot* | pilot |
| le pinceau | *luh pa(n)-saw* | paintbrush |
| le pique-nique | *luh peek-neek* | picnic |
| la piscine | *la pee-seen* | swimming pool |
| la piste | *la peest* | runway |
| la pizza | *la peetza* | pizza |
| le placard | *luh pla-kahr* | closet |
| le plafond | *luh pla-fo(n)* | ceiling |
| la plage | *la plaj* | beach |
| la planche | *la plo(n)sh* | plank |
| la planche à repasser | *la plo(n)sh a ruh-passai* | ironing board |
| la planche à roulettes | *la plo(n)sh a roollett* | skateboard |
| la planche à voile | *la plo(n)sh a vwal* | windsurfing |
| le plancher | *luh plo(n)shai* | floor |
| la planète | *la pla-net* | planet |
| la plante | *la plo(n)t* | plant |
| le plateau | *luh pla-taw* | tray |
| la plate-bande | *la platt-bo(n)d* | flower bed |
| le plâtre | *luh platr* | cast |
| plein | *pla(n)* | full |
| pleurer | *pluh-rai* | to cry |
| le plongeon | *luh plo(n)-jo(n)* | diving |
| la pluie | *la plwee* | rain |
| la plume | *la plewm* | feather |
| le pneu | *luh p-nuh* | tire |
| la poche | *la posh* | pocket |
| la poêle | *la pwal* | frying pan |
| la poignée | *la pwan-yai* | door handle |
| la poire | *la pwar* | pear |
| le poireau | *luh pwa-ro* | leek |
| le poisson | *luh pwa-so(n)* | fish |
| le poisson rouge | *luh pwa-so(n) rooj* | goldfish |
| la poitrine | *la pwa-treen* | chest (body) |
| le poivre | *luh pwavr* | pepper |

| | | |
|---|---|---|
| la pomme | *la pom* | apple |
| la pomme de terre | *la pom duh tair* | potato |
| la pompe à essence | *la po(m)pa esso(n)ss* | gas pump |
| le pompier | *luh po(m)p-yai* | fireman |
| le poney | *luh ponnai* | pony |
| le pont | *luh po(n)* | bridge |
| le pop-corn | *luh pop-korn* | popcorn |
| la porcherie | *la por-shuh-ree* | pigsty |
| la porte | *la port* | door |
| le portemanteau | *luh port-mo(n)taw* | peg (for clothes) |
| le porte-monnaie | *luh port monnai* | purse |
| porter | *portai* | to carry |
| le poster | *luh poss-tair* | poster |
| le pot de peinture | *luh po duh pa(n)tewr* | paint can |
| le poteau indicateur | *luh po-taw a(n)deeka-ter* | signpost |
| le pot | *luh po* | jar |
| la poubelle | *la poobell* | trash can |
| le pouce | *luh pooss* | thumb |
| le poulailler | *luh poo-lie-yai* | hen house |
| la poule | *la pool* | hen |
| le poulet | *luh poollai* | chicken |
| la poupée | *la poo-pai* | doll |
| pousser | *poossai* | to push |
| la poussette | *la poossett* | stroller |
| le poussin | *luh poossa(n)* | chick |
| premier | *pruhm-yai* | first |
| prendre | *pro(n)dr* | to take |
| près | *prai* | near |
| le printemps | *luh pra(n)-to(m)* | spring (season) |
| propre | *propr* | clean |
| la prune | *la prewn* | plum |
| le pull-over | *luh pewllo-vair* | sweater |
| la punaise | *la pewnaiz* | thumb tack |
| la purée | *la pew-rai* | mashed potatoes |
| le puzzle | *luh puhzl* | jigsaw |
| le pyjama | *luh pee-jamma* | pajamas |

## Q

| | | |
|---|---|---|
| le quai | *luh kai* | platform |
| quatorze | *ka-torz* | fourteen |
| quatre | *katr* | four |
| la queue | *la kuh* | tail |
| quinze | *ka(n)z* | fifteen |

## R

| | | |
|---|---|---|
| le rabot | *luh ra-bo* | (wood) plane |
| le radiateur | *luh rad-yat-er* | radiator |
| la radio | *la rad-yo* | radio |
| les rails (m) | *lai rye* | train track |
| le raisin | *luh raiza(n)* | grapes |
| la rame | *la ram* | oar |
| ramper | *ro(m)pai* | to crawl |
| rapide | *ra-peed* | fast |
| la raquette | *la ra-ket* | racket |
| le râteau | *luh ra-to* | rake |
| le rectangle | *luh rek-to(n)gl* | rectangle |
| le réfrigérateur | *luh rai-free-jaira-ter* | refrigerator |
| regarder | *ruh-ga-rdai* | to watch, to look |
| la règle | *la raigl* | ruler |
| la remorque | *la ruh-mork* | trailer |
| le renard | *luh ruh-nar* | fox |
| le renardeau | *luh ruh-nar-do* | fox cub |
| le renne | *luh renn* | reindeer |
| le requin | *luh ruh-ka(n)* | shark |
| le rhinocéros | *luh reenno-saiross* | rhinoceros |
| le rideau | *luh ree-do* | curtain |
| rire | *reer* | to laugh |
| la rivière | *la reev-yair* | river |

| French | Pronunciation | English |
|---|---|---|
| riz | luh ree | rice |
| robe | la rob | dress |
| robe de chambre | la rob duh sho(m)br | bathrobe |
| robinet | luh robbee-nai | faucet |
| robot | luh robbo | robot |
| rocher | luh ro-shai | rock |
| rollers (m) | lai rollair | roller blades |
| rondin | luh ro(n)da(n) | log |
| se | roz | pink |
| rosée | la ro-zai | dew |
| roue | la roo | wheel |
| ge | rooj | red |
| rouleau compresseur | luh roo-lo ko(m)press-er | steamroller |
| route | la root | road |
| ruban | luh rewbo(n) | ribbon |
| ruche | la rewsh | beehive |
| rue | la rew | street |
| rugby | luh rewg-bee | rugby |
| ruisseau | luh rwee-saw | stream |
| | | |
| sable | luh sabl | sand |
| sac | luh sak | sack, carrier bag |
| sac à dos | luh sakka-daw | backpack |
| sac à main | luh sakka-ma(n) | purse |
| saison | la saizo(n) | season |
| salade | la sa-lad | lettuce |
| le | sal | dirty |
| salle d'attente | la sal da-to(n)t | waiting room |
| salle de bains | la sal duh ba(n) | bathroom |
| salon | luh sa-lo(n) | living room |
| medi | sam-dee | Saturday |
| sandale | la so(n)-dal | sandal |
| sandwich | luh so(n)d-weech | sandwich |
| sapin de Noël | luh sa-pa(n) duh no-ell | Christmas tree |
| saucisse | la saw-seess | sausage |
| saucisson | luh saw-see-so(n) | salami |
| uter | saw-tai | to jump |
| uter à la corde | saw-tai alla kord | to skip |
| savon | luh sah-vo(n) | soap |
| scie | la see | saw |
| sciure | la see-ewr | sawdust |
| seau | luh saw | bucket |
| bagarrer | suh ba-garrai | to fight |
| c | sek | dry |
| cacher | suh ka-shai | to hide |
| ze | saiz | sixteen |
| sel | luh sell | salt |
| laver | suh la-vai | to wash |
| selle | la sell | saddle |
| ot | sett | seven |
| seringue | la suh-ra(n)g | syringe |
| serpent | luh sair-po(n) | snake |
| serre | la sair | greenhouse |
| serveur | luh sairv-er | waiter |
| serveuse | la sair-verz | waitress |
| serviette | la sairv-yet | towel |
| short | luh shorrt | shorts |
| sifflet | luh see-flai | whistle |
| singe | luh sa(n)j | monkey |
| | seess | six |
| ski | luh skee | ski |
| ski nautique | luh skee nawteek | water skiing |
| slip | luh sleep | underwear |
| soeur | la ser | sister |
| soir | luh swar | evening |
| soldat de plomb | luh sol-da duh plo(m) | tin soldier |
| soleil | luh so-lay | sun |

| French | Pronunciation | English |
|---|---|---|
| sombre | so(m)br | dark |
| la soucoupe | la soo-koop | saucer |
| souffler | soo-flai | to blow |
| la soupe | la soop | soup |
| le sourcil | luh soor-see | eyebrow |
| sourire | sooreer | to smile |
| la souris | la soo-ree | mouse |
| sous | soo | under |
| le sous-marin | luh soo-ma-ra(n) | submarine |
| les spaghetti (m) | lai spa-gettee | spaghetti |
| le sport | luh spor | sport |
| le steward | luh stew-ard | flight attendant |
| le store | luh stor | (window) blind |
| le stylo à encre | luh stee-lo a o(n)kr | fountain pen |
| le sucre | luh sewkr | sugar |
| le sumo | luh sewmo | sumo wrestling |
| sur | sewr | over |
| le surf de neige | luh suhrf duh naij | snowboarding |
| le sweat-shirt | luh sweat-shirrt | sweatshirt |

## T

| French | Pronunciation | English |
|---|---|---|
| la table | la tabl | table |
| le tableau | luh ta-blaw | board |
| le tableau noir | luh ta-blaw nwar | blackboard |
| le tablier | luh ta-blee-ai | apron |
| le tabouret | luh ta-boo-rai | stool |
| le tambour | luh to(m)-boor | drum |
| les tampons (m) | lai to(m)-po(n) | buffers |
| la tante | la to(n)t | aunt |
| la tasse | la tass | cup |
| la taupe | la tawp | mole |
| le taureau | luh taw-raw | bull |
| le taxi | luh ta-xee | taxi |
| le tee-shirt | luh tee-shirrt | T-shirt |
| le téléphone | luh tellai-fon | telephone |
| le télescope | luh tellai-skop | telescope |
| le télésiège | luh tellaiss-yaij | chairlift |
| la télévision | la tellai-veez-yo(n) | television |
| le temps | luh to(m) | weather |
| le tennis | luh tenneess | tennis |
| le tennis de table | luh tenneess duh tabl | table tennis |
| la tente | la to(n)t | aunt |
| la terre | la tair | dirt |
| le têtard | luh tai-tar | tadpole |
| la tête | la tait | head |
| le thé | luh tai | tea |
| le thermomètre | luh tair-mo-maitr | thermometer |
| le tigre | luh teegr | tiger |
| le tir à la carabine | luh teer alla ka-ra-been | rifle range |
| le tir à l'arc | luh teer allark | archery |
| tirer | teerai | to pull |
| la tirelire | la teer-leer | money box |
| le tiroir | luh teerwar | drawer |
| le toboggan | luh to-bo-go(n) | slide |
| le tobaggan géant | luh to-bo-go(n) jai-o(n) | giant slide |
| la toile d'araignée | la twall da-renn-yai | cobweb |
| les toilettes (f) | lai twa-lett | toilet |
| le toit | luh twa | roof |
| la tomate | la to-mat | tomato |
| tomber | to(m)-bai | to fall |
| la tondeuse | la to(n)-derz | lawn mower |
| le tonneau | luh tonnaw | barrel |
| le torchon | luh tor-shon | dish towel |
| la tortue | la tor-tew | tortoise |
| la tour de contrôle | la toor duh ko(n)trawl | control tower |
| le tournevis | luh toor-nuh-veess | screwdriver |
| le tourniquet | luh toor-neekai | sprinkler |
| le tracteur | luh trak-ter | tractor |

| | | |
|---|---|---|
| le train | *luh tra(n)* | train |
| le train de marchandises | *luh tra(n) duh mar-sho(n)-deez* | freight train |
| le train électrique | *luh tra(n) ellek-treek* | train set |
| le traîneau | *luh trai-naw* | sleigh |
| le train fantôme | *luh tra(n) fo(n)tawm* | ghost train (ride) |
| le transat | *luh tro(n)-zat* | deck chair |
| le trapèze | *luh tra-paiz* | trapeze |
| treize | *traiz* | thirteen |
| le triangle | *luh tree-o(n)gl* | triangle |
| le tricycle | *luh tree-seekl* | tricycle |
| tricoter | *tree-kottai* | to knit |
| trois | *trwa* | three |
| la trompe | *la tro(m)p* | trunk |
| la trompette | *la tro(m)-pet* | trumpet |
| le trottoir | *luh tro-twar* | pavement |
| le trou | *luh troo* | hole |
| le tunnel | *luh tew-nell* | tunnel |
| le tuyau | *luh twee-yaw* | pipe |
| le tuyau d'arrosage | *luh twee-yaw da-ro-zaj* | hose |

## U

| | | |
|---|---|---|
| un | *a(n)* | one |
| l'usine (f) | *lew-zeen* | factory |

## V

| | | |
|---|---|---|
| les vacances (f) | *lai va-ko(n)ss* | vacation |
| la vache | *la vash* | cow |
| la vague | *la vag* | wave |
| le vaisseau spatial | *luh vai-saw spa-see-al* | spaceship |
| la valise | *la va-leez* | suitcase |
| le veau | *luh vaw* | calf |
| vendredi | *vo(n)-druh-dee* | Friday |
| le vent | *luh vo(n)* | wind |
| le ventre | *luh vo(n)tr* | tummy |
| le ver de terre | *luh vair duh tair* | worm |
| le verger | *luh vair-jai* | orchard |
| le verre | *luh vair* | glass |
| vert | *vair* | green |
| le vestiaire | *luh vest-yair* | changing room |
| les vêtements (m) | *lai vait-mo(n)* | clothes |
| le/la vétérinaire | *luh/la vettaireenair* | vet (man/woman) |
| la viande | *la vee-o(n)d* | meat |
| vide | *veed* | empty |
| vieux | *vee-yuh* | old |
| violet | *vee-olai* | purple |
| le village | *luh vee-laj* | village, town |
| vingt | *va(n)* | twenty |
| la vis | *la veess* | screw |
| vivant | *vee-vo(n)* | alive |
| la voile | *la vwal* | sailing |
| la voiture | *la vwa-tewr* | car |
| la voiture de course | *la vwa-tewr duh koorss* | racing car |
| la voiture de police | *la vwa-tewr duh po-leess* | police car |
| le voyage | *luh vwa-yaj* | trip |

## W

| | | |
|---|---|---|
| le wagon | *luh va-go(n)* | railway car |

## Y

| | | |
|---|---|---|
| le yaourt | *luh ya-oort* | yogurt |

## Z

| | | |
|---|---|---|
| le zèbre | *luh zaibr* | zebra |
| le zoo | *luh zo-o* | zoo |

ISBN 0-590-92178-9

Copyright © 1979, 1995 by Usborne Publishing Ltd. All rights reserved. Published by Scholastic Inc., 555 Broadway, New York, NY 10012, by arrangement with Usborne Publishing Ltd.

12 11 10 9 8 7 6 5 4 3 2 1     6 7 8 9/9 0 1/0

Printed in the U.S.A.     08

First Scholastic printing, September 1996